D0484408

The Mystery
of the
Magi

The Mystery of the Magi

DANIEL KOLENDA
WITH ROBERT GLADSTONE

CHRIST
FOR ALL NATIONS

THE MYSTERY OF THE MAGI

© 2018 by Daniel Kolenda

Published by Christ for all Nations
PO Box 590588
Orlando, FL 32859-0588
CfaN.org

ISBN: 978-1-933446-60-8

Edited by PrimeDoor Media and Marketing
PrimeDoor.org

Interior Design by JoshType.com
Cover Design by DesignstoGo.net

Printed in the United States of America

TABLE OF CONTENTS

Now after Jesus was born in Bethlehem of Judea in the days of Herod the king, magi from the east arrived in Jerusalem, saying, "Where is He who has been born King of the Jews? For we saw His star in the east and have come to worship Him."

Matthew 2:1-2

SECTION I:

WHY IS CHRISTMAS IMPORTANT?

A few days before Christmas, I was walking through the mall. The hustle and bustle of last minute shoppers filled the air like bees buzzing around their hive. I had joined the swarm of consumers on the hunt for the final few gifts to complete my shopping list, when suddenly I heard something: a familiar melody floating through the air carrying the most pristine doctrine. The song broadcasted a message of ultimate truth at odds with the mall's busy consumerism. For most people, the message went completely unnoticed. It was simply more noise droning in the background. But for me, it cut through the clamor, arrested my attention and struck me in an unexpected way.

Recently, there had been yet another shooting in which a young African-American man was killed by a police officer. Racial tension was high, debates raged and riots broke out across the country. The incident was just the latest in a series of ongoing conflicts in our nation, but really it was just one recent example of a scandal raging since the Garden of Eden.

What can be done about the problems in our world: fear, hatred, racism, violence, pain, suffering, death and evil? There seems to be no solution. Our amazing advances in technology, medicine, philosophy and science have cured many symptoms, but they have not touched the underlying disease. The protests and riots I had seen on the news earlier that day seemed like overflowing frustrations toward a problem no one knows how to solve.

And then there it was—the answer to the problem playing over a sound system in a crowded shopping mall. It rang out like an anthem in the last place you would expect. I stood still in the middle of the aisle, between the radio-controlled cars and Barbie dolls, and listened. I wondered why no one else was getting it. Tears welled up in my eyes as I was awed by the power of the words:

"Truly He taught us to love one another,
His law is love and His gospel is peace.
Chains shall He break for the slave is our brother
And in His name all oppression shall cease.
Sweet hymns of joy in grateful chorus raise we,
Let all within us praise His holy name.
Christ is the Lord, oh,
Praise His name forever
His power and glory ever more proclaim!
His power and glory ever more proclaim!"
("O Holy Night" Adolphe Adam, 1847)

Given the level of darkness descending on our world, one might think that any redemptive Christmas message would have been lost long ago: silenced by secular culture, emasculated by political correctness, ridiculed by humanism and drowned out by materialism (especially this time of year). Yet there it was, the Gospel, the remedy for the human condition, disguised as a harmless Christmas carol in a shopping mall.

This is one reason that Christmas is my favorite time of the year. I love the lights and tinsel, the comfort of a steaming cup of hot chocolate and the way a cozy fire calls everyone around the hearth. I love the way we all become more aware of what is really important in life: family, kindness, peace, love and joy. Even in the secular world, there seems to be a consciousness of something transcendent and divine during this time of year. But most of all, I love the fact that at Christmas, the Gospel rings out across the world as angels announce the birth of a Savior and shepherds worship a newborn King.

On Christmas day, even among the most secular, the most heathen, the most godless in our society, almost everyone will pause. Even the biggest retail chains will close for one day. Parking lots will be empty, and people will be home with whatever family they have. The world will stand still for 24 hours as a strange moment of silence settles over the earth. It is absolutely remarkable and profound.

PEACE ON EARTH

An astonishing example of this happened in 1914. The world was in the midst of one of the bloodiest and most horrific wars in history. During World War I, powerful new weapons were introduced to old-fashioned battlefields, and the carnage was unimaginable. Trenches where the soldiers fought were hell on earth. At times, the dead were piled six feet high. But on Christmas Eve of the war's first year, something amazing happened. German and British troops began singing Christmas carols to one another from their trenches. The next day, as the light of dawn broke across the horizon, these mortal enemies shouted, "Merry Christmas!" in each other's native languages. Then, a truly surreal event took place. The soldiers emerged from their protective trenches and began to shake hands and exchange gifts. They played friendly games of soccer, ate meals and sang together. The war had not ended, but somehow, in the midst of a human hell, there was a moment of peace on earth, good will to men.

One could be tempted to dismiss a story like this as sappy Christmas sentimentalism, but it is not obvious that such stories should exist. There are many holidays that celebrate countless lives, but one life stands above all the rest. Only His day could affect the globe so dramatically even among unbelievers. The Apostle John said that this life, the life of Jesus, was the light of men (John 1:4). In John's day, no one could have imagined how accurate that statement would be.

The life of Jesus is truly the light of humanity. He stands like a sparkling diamond among the dark coals of human history. His life has brought light to an otherwise bleak and hopeless world. If you could view the timeline of human existence all at once, there would be one mark that shines as bright as the Star of Bethlehem: the life of that humble carpenter from Nazareth.

His life split time in two. Those before Him looked ahead in anticipation of His coming, and those after

Him look back in reverent awe. We even talk about history in terms of Before Christ (B.C.) and Anno Domini (A.D.), "The year of our Lord." He marked the end of one era and the beginning of another, both literally and figuratively.

Because of Jesus, humanity has been immeasurably blessed. For example, care for the sick and mentally ill spread across the world as a result of Christianity. The teachings of Jesus led to the concepts of women's rights, abolition of slavery and care for the poor. He is the light of society, literature, philosophy, history, spirituality and all of human existence.

American Evangelist Billy Sunday said, "When the bright cloud hid Him from the gaze of those who loved Him with a devotion that took them to martyrdom, the only record of His sayings was graven upon their hearts, but now libraries are devoted to the consideration of them. No words were ever so weighty or so weighed as those of Him who was so poor that

He had nowhere to lay His head. The scholarship of the world has sat at His feet with bared head, and has been compelled to say again and again, 'Never man spake as He spake.' His utterances have been translated into every known tongue, and have carried healing on their wings wherever they have gone. No other book has ever had a tithe of the circulation of that which contains His words, and not only that, but His thoughts and the story of His life are so interwoven in all literature that if a man should never read a line in the Bible, and yet be a reader at all he could not remain ignorant of the Christ."

No wonder the world stands still on the day we remember His birth. His life is like the sun in the Milky Way. Its influence is so massive the whole world revolves around it, even when we are not aware of it. It is at Christmas that His influence seems more vivid than usual. The Gospel rings out from every carol and cantata, from every card and nativity scene. How I want the world to understand the power of what these things convey!

Sages, leave your contemplations,
Brighter visions beam afar;
Seek the great desire of nations,
Ye have seen His natal star;
Come and worship,
Come and worship,
Worship Christ, the newborn King!

("Angels from the Realms of Glory"
James Montgomery, 1816)

SECTION II:

BEYOND THE NATIVITY SCENE

How strange the "Nativity Scene" must look to someone who doesn't understand it. It is a portrayal of Christ's birth that blends elements from two Gospels and adds some traditional, and a few mistaken, details. It usually shows Mary and Joseph looking after their baby lying on a trough filled with hay. Shepherds and three "kings" kneel before them, with the "kings" offering special gifts. Camels and other animals surround the little group on the ground, while a bright star and angels frame it above.

So, this traditional nativity scene points beyond itself, signifying there is much more to the story it depicts. This book will focus on one part of the story that is very mysterious, highly unusual, but also deeply compelling: the arrival of the "wise men," also known as the "Magi." Their association with Christ's birth almost seems out of place. Only Matthew's Gospel mentions their visit. He gives no explanation or background to the Magi, yet there is a clear prophetic significance to their presence. They connect with something from the past, announce something about the present and predict something in the future.

In popular nativity scenes, the Magi have been portrayed as three camel-riding kings who attended the birth of Christ along with the shepherds and barnyard animals; but, we know from Scripture that several aspects of this traditional folklore are incorrect. First, the Magi were not kings. The word "Magi" refers to pagan astrologers from the East who sought knowledge from the stars and planets and interpreted dreams. Second, the Magi did not join the shepherds to visit Jesus on the day of His birth. They came on a separate occasion.[1] Finally, the Bible never specifies that there were only three Magi. We know their caravan was large, because all of Jerusalem knew when they entered town (Matt 2:3,) but we do not know exactly how many there were.

---

[1] The shepherds visited Jesus immediately after His birth (Luke 2:11-16), while the Magi visited sometime after his birth (Matt 2:2), up to two years later (Matt 2:16).

What intrigue they bring to the Christmas story! Rather than, as the song says, "We three kings of orient are...," these strange stargazers came from foreign places to seek the Jewish King. Do we know anything about them? How did a star guide them to this special Child? Why would they dare to call Him "King of the Jews," confirming their praise with extravagant gifts? What was the significance of those specific gifts? Answers to these questions reveal a crucial, but often-neglected, aspect of the Christmas story: The Mystery of the Magi.

THE ORIGINAL "WISE MEN"

The only other book in the Bible to mention "Magi" is Daniel. About 600 years before Christ, the Babylonians started to take captive Jews into exile. A young Hebrew named Daniel was among the first to go, and his story in Babylon is where the Bible introduces us to the Magi.

Daniel's life is fascinating because of the extraordinary extent to which revelatory dreams and supernatural prophetic activity opened doors for him. As a man with the prophetic Spirit, Daniel became influential in the highest places of power, even advising the ruler of Babylon, King Nebuchadnezzar, himself.

One night, that king had a dream:

"Now in the second year of Nebuchadnezzar's reign, Nebuchadnezzar had dreams; and his spirit was so troubled that his sleep left him. Then the king gave the command to call the magicians, the astrologers [in Greek, "magi"], the sorcerers, and the Chaldeans to tell the king his dreams. So, they came and stood before the king. And the king said to them, 'I have had a dream, and my spirit is anxious to know the dream.' Then the Chaldeans spoke to the king in Aramaic, 'O king, live forever! Tell your servants the dream, and we will give the interpretation.' The king answered and said to the Chaldeans, 'My decision is firm: if you do not make known the dream to me, and its interpretation, you shall be cut in pieces, and your houses shall be made an ash

heap. However, if you tell the dream and its interpretation,
you shall receive from me gifts, rewards, and great honor.
Therefore, tell me the dream and its interpretation.'"

–Daniel 2:1-6

This passage mentions the Magi for the first time in
Scripture. They appeared in King Nebuchadnezzar's
court when he called his spiritual advisors to decipher
his mysterious dream. In the Greek translation of
the Old Testament, those called "astrologers" above
are the Magi. Theirs was one of four groups called
together to create the king's spiritual advisory board.
The king was serious about getting the authoritative
interpretation to his dream, so he put them to the test.
Any pretender could fabricate an interpretation for
a dream, but if these groups truly had supernatural
insight, they would have to demonstrate it. If they
could first tell the king his dream, then he would
believe their interpretation. Unfortunately, each of the
four groups, including the Magi, failed. So, in his fury,
the king planned to kill them.

"For this reason the king was angry and very furious, and gave the command to destroy all the wise men of Babylon. So the decree went out, and they began killing the wise men; and they sought Daniel and his companions, to kill them. Then with counsel and wisdom Daniel answered Arioch, the captain of the king's guard, who had gone out to kill the wise men of Babylon; he answered and said to Arioch the king's captain, 'Why is the decree from the king so urgent?' Then Arioch made the decision known to Daniel. So Daniel went in and asked the king to give him time, that he might tell the king the interpretation. Then Daniel went to his house, and made the decision known to Hananiah, Mishael, and Azariah, his companions, that they might seek mercies from the God of heaven concerning this secret, so that Daniel and his companions might not perish with the rest of the wise men of Babylon. Then the secret was revealed to Daniel in a night vision. So Daniel blessed the God of heaven."

                                                    —Daniel 2:12-19

DANIEL'S LEADERSHIP
AND LEGACY IN BABYLON

Of all the wise men in Babylon, no one had the power to discern the king's dream except for Daniel, the Lord's prophet from Judea. After Daniel told the king his dream and its interpretation, Nebuchadnezzar promoted him to a high rank of political authority that included jurisdiction over all the wise men of Babylon, including the Magi.

"Then King Nebuchadnezzar fell on his face, prostrate before Daniel, and commanded that they should present an offering and incense to him. The king answered Daniel, and said, 'Truly your God is the God of gods, the Lord of kings, and a revealer of secrets, since you could reveal this secret.' Then the king promoted Daniel and gave him many great gifts; and he made him ruler over the whole province of Babylon, and chief administrator over all the wise men of Babylon. Also Daniel petitioned the king, and he set Shadrach, Meshach, and Abednego over the affairs of the province of Babylon; but Daniel sat in the gate of the king." —Daniel 2:46-49

Some of the "wise men" in Daniel's charge were the predecessors of the Magi we see hundreds of years later in the Gospel of Matthew, traveling from the East to worship Jesus. They had a revelation from God and came to Jerusalem to honor the true King. Yet, their pedigree was decidedly heathen. The "wise men" in Daniel's day were pagan astrologers and diviners and even practiced magic and fortunetelling. But can you see God at work? He sent a true prophet to these false prophets! Because God used Daniel to give a powerful revelation to King Nebuchadnezzar, he rose to the place of influence over these practitioners of false religion and dark arts. God sent His witness into this dark corner of the world to shine the light of His Kingdom. As Matthew's Christmas story shows us, Daniel's light in Babylon became a legacy for the Magi's descendants. It began a story that would become a great prophetic sign to Israel and the world.

Daniel was placed over the pagan mystics of Babylon, surely becoming a teacher and mentor to many of them. After all, these "wise men" were supposed to be experts in the spiritual realm with the ability to interpret signs and predict the future. Daniel's clear prophetic superiority demanded their deepest respect. His influence was so valuable that he continued in this role through the reign of Belshazzar, the son of Nebuchadnezzar. Then, after Babylon was conquered, Daniel continued to serve the next empire under Darius the Mede and Cyrus the Persian king.

Even though he was a foreigner, four kings from two empires elevated Daniel to some of the highest places of power in the world. Daniel was an extraordinary man. Both his excellent character and astonishing abilities opened supernatural doors of favor for him. His exploits were legendary. His unique Jewish faith, teachings and prophecies must have fascinated those under his influence. Undoubtedly, the very writings we have in the book of Daniel became holy texts for some of those eastern mystics, the Magi. In fact, along with several other prophetic visions and interpretations, Daniel foretold the coming of the Jewish Messiah. That prophecy became part of the written inheritance Daniel left for his spiritual descendants, including some of the wise men from Babylon and Persia.

"Seventy weeks are determined for your people and for your holy city, to finish the transgression, to make an end of sins, to make reconciliation for iniquity, to bring in everlasting righteousness, to seal up vision and prophecy, and to anoint the Most Holy. Know therefore and understand, that from the going forth of the command to restore and build Jerusalem until Messiah the Prince, there shall be seven weeks and sixty-two weeks; the street shall be built again, and the wall, even in troublesome times. And after the sixty-two weeks Messiah shall be cut off, but not for Himself; and the people of the prince who is to come shall destroy the city and the sanctuary. The end of it shall be with a flood, and till the end of the war desolations are determined. Then he shall confirm a covenant with many for one week; but in the middle of the week he shall bring an end to sacrifice and offering. And on

the wing of abominations shall be one who makes desolate,
even until the consummation, which is determined, is poured
out on the desolate."   *–Daniel 9:24-27*

Not only did Daniel foretell the coming of the
Messiah, but he also gave a precise prediction for
when the Messiah would die and what He would
accomplish. For example, Daniel declared the Messiah
would "make an end of sin" and "bring in everlasting
righteousness." Eventually He would die, be "cut
off," but not for Himself. Daniel's prophecies were
so precise that he accurately foretold the very day of
Jesus' Triumphal Entry hundreds of years before Jesus
was even born![2]

---

[2] Daniel 9:25 says that it would be "seven weeks and sixty-two weeks"
unto "Messiah the Prince." (A week is 7 days, so if you take 7 x 69 years
= 483 years.) Jews and Babylonians at that time counted 360 days per
year. So, 483 years, at 360 days per year = 173,880 days. The prophecy
says that the days would start counting down "…from the command to
restore and build Jerusalem." This happened in Nehemiah 2:1-8 when
Artaxerxes gave the command to rebuild Jerusalem on March 14, 445
BC. If we count 173,880 days from this date (correcting for leap years)
we come to April 6, 32 A.D., the day Jesus made His triumphal entry
into Jerusalem and revealed Himself as Messiah in exactly the way
Zechariah predicted he would (Zechariah 9:9).

Daniel also prophesied many future events in the Gentile world with astonishing accuracy. For example, he predicted the rise of the Medo-Persian, Greek and Roman empires in their proper order. He gave detailed descriptions of the way many important, historical events would unfold. It is quite possible that future generations of Magi came to appreciate Daniel's prophetic gift even more than his contemporaries. As they watched prophecy after prophecy come to pass over the years, they must have grown increasingly confident that Daniel had indeed possessed divine knowledge of the future. Perhaps there was a revival of interest in the prophecies of Daniel among the Magi of Persia as 600 years of fulfilled predictions brought them to the time of the greatest fulfillment of all: the birth of the Messiah.

Daniel had prophesied that the coming Messiah would be a great king, so when the Magi arrived in Judea, they started at the logical place; they went to the king's palace.

Then let us all with one accord
Sing praises to our heavenly Lord;
That hath made heaven and earth of naught,
And with his blood mankind hath bought

("The First Noel" Unknown Author, 17th century)

SECTION III:

NATIONS WILL FLOW TO ZION

The Roman Senate had named Herod the Great, who was ruling over Judea, "king of the Jews," but he was just a puppet of the Roman Empire. He had no rightful claim to the throne of David. Like most rulers of his day, Herod was paranoid and superstitious. So, when eastern astrologers showed up claiming that a star led them to Judea in search of a Child prophesied to be "King of the Jews," Herod could not have felt more threatened. He was determined to find and murder this baby. So, he called his own "wise men," Jewish chief priests and scribes, and learned from them exactly where the Messiah would be born.

Now this is amazing. Herod asked Jewish priests and scribes to find the specific place of Messiah's birth. Consulting the Hebrew Scriptures, they gave him the precise location. How could they know where their own Messiah had been born and yet seem totally disinterested?

What's more, Jesus was no longer an infant by this point. He could have been as much as two years old (Matthew 2:16). Surely there were rumors of His birth throughout Israel. Luke says that the shepherds "made widely known" what they had seen and heard (Luke 2:17). Anna and Simeon had both received divine confirmation that Jesus was the Christ. Word was undoubtedly spreading. These rumblings, combined with the direct knowledge from Scripture, should have caused all Israel to look for this newborn King. Yet no kings, priests, scribes or religious leaders in Israel acknowledged Him. None of them bothered to seek Him, much less worship Him. The Jewish leadership seemed totally disinterested.

Keep in mind that these religious leaders were also politicians. Their prosperity and the security of their positions were ensured by the current Roman administration. Herod was their king. As long as he guaranteed their continued prosperity, they wanted no other leader. The common people might have welcomed a Messiah, but those with position and power would have considered Him a threat. Messiah meant revolution, disturbing the status quo and endangering their profitable arrangement. No wonder Matthew tells us that, when Herod heard of the Magi's search for another Jewish king, "He was troubled, *and all Jerusalem with him*" (Matthew 2:3, my emphasis).

Despite the shameful neglect by the establishment in Jerusalem, God had already set a process in motion to honor the royalty of His Son. Six hundred years earlier, under Daniel's leadership, pagan "wise men," including a group of Magi, began to learn about the Jewish Messiah's advent and mission. After centuries of changing empires, that legacy culminated in Magi traveling from the East to worship Jesus with precious gifts and to acknowledge Him as King.

In telling us this story, Matthew illustrated a pattern that would repeat throughout the life and ministry of the Messiah. "He came to His own, and His own did not receive Him" (John 1:11). He was without honor in his own country (Luke 4:24). He was the "stone which the builders rejected" (Matthew 21:42, Mark 12:10). He was ultimately spurned and killed by His own people. All of this fulfilled the prophetic Scriptures about the Messiah.

Matthew also expected his readers to catch the striking irony: Gentile astrologers discovered the Jewish King by following a star, but the scholars of Israel failed to discern their King while possessing the Scriptures. Pagan Magi came to worship the Messiah, but Jerusalem royalty sought to kill Him. The contrast was sharp, startling and prophetic.

These Magi were the first Gentiles to worship the Jewish Messiah as King, even when the religious establishment had rejected Him, but they were only the beginning. Later, Gentiles would come to Him by the millions and even billions. That was always God's intention. Thus, at the end of Matthew's Gospel, King

Jesus commanded His followers to make disciples "of all the nations" (Matthew 28:19). Then, the last book of the Bible reveals the end result. The legacy that began with Daniel's ministry, as far back as the ancient Babylonian empire, then became a trickle of Magi from the East to worship Jesus, eventually culminating in a deluge of multitudes from every nation under heaven.

"After these things I looked, and behold, a great multitude which no one could number, of all nations, tribes, peoples, and tongues, standing before the throne and before the Lamb, clothed with white robes, with palm branches in their hands, and crying out with a loud voice, saying, 'Salvation belongs to our God who sits on the throne, and to the Lamb!'" —Revelation 7:9, 10

The message of the Magi declares that the Jewish Messiah is the Lord of all nations. God has provided the way to save *all* who believe. One day, people from every tribe, kindred, and tongue will gather as one family to confess that Jesus Christ is Lord, to the glory of God the Father.

GOD CHOOSES THE WEAK TO SHAME THE STRONG

The story of the Magi communicates another striking truth. God delights to use the most unlikely people and unexpected situations to accomplish His purposes. He breaks every human convention and protocol. He sent His Son, not as a conquering warrior, but as a helpless baby. He was not born to a princess living in a palace, but to a peasant virgin in a barn. His birth was not attended by royal emissaries, but by shepherds. He was not honored by the spiritual leaders and scholars of His own people, but by pagan astrologers from the Gentile world. So, why does God operate this way? He "has chosen what is insignificant and despised in the world – what is viewed as nothing – to bring to nothing what is viewed as something, so that no one may boast in His presence" (1 Corinthians 1:28-29, CSB).

Today, most of the world celebrates the birth of Jesus in December, and every year a few Christians protest. They point out, correctly, that Jesus was not born in December. Then they draw the historical connection between that date and ancient pagan winter celebrations. But I will tell you why this does not bother me. If we really celebrate Christ's birth during a time once used as a pagan holiday, then that seems to fit the narrative of Christ's birth quite appropriately. God will use the most unusual things and people to bring glory to His Son. Nothing about the birth of Jesus fit conventional or traditional dogmas. After all, would mainstream religion have predicted that Gentile, pagan astrologers would be among the first to worship the King of the Jews and Son of the Most High God? The Magi of Matthew's Gospel may not have been natural candidates for our nativity scenes, but they were natural candidates in God's. I would be happy if every pagan holiday became a celebration of the One who is Lord over every day of the week, month and year.

When Jesus made His "Triumphal Entry" into Jerusalem, the people praised God in loud voices and recognized Jesus as Messiah. The jealous Pharisees demanded that Jesus rebuke the disciples for their outburst. In response, Jesus said, "I tell you that if these should keep silent, the stones would immediately cry out" (Luke 19:40). It seems that the Father will not allow His Son to go unrecognized and unpraised. If people won't praise Him, inanimate objects will. If the Jewish "wise men" won't praise Him, pagan wise men will. One way or another, God will get His glory.

There's a song in the air,
There's a star in the sky;
There's a mother's deep prayer
And a baby's low cry;

There's a tumult of joy
O'er the wonderful birth,
For the virgin's sweet boy
Is the Lord of the Earth.

And the star rains its fire,
And the beautiful sing
for the Manger of Bethlehem cradles a King;

("There's A Star in the Sky" J.G. Holland, 1872)

SECTION IV:

THE STAR

"When they heard the king, they departed; and behold, the star which they had seen in the East went before them, till it came and stood over where the young Child was."

−Matthew 2:9

M any theories have been suggested about what the Magi actually saw in the sky over Israel. Some have speculated it may have been a concurrence of bright stars, a comet or a supernova. But in my opinion, explanations based on strictly natural phenomena fall short, and I will explain why.

If the Magi's star was a natural star, it would have had to defy the laws of physics. The movement of stars usually traverse the sky from east to west. But the "star" the Magi saw led them from Jerusalem to Bethlehem, moving north to south. Furthermore, the star led them to the precise location of a certain individual house, which of course a heavenly body, millions of light years from earth, could not do. The Bible even says that when the star came to the place where the Child was, it "stood still," something stars do not do. There is definitely something unusual about this star.

The Scripture doesn't explain exactly how this star was able to behave in such a unique and unprecedented way. Since we are left to speculate, I might as well give a theory of my own. It is possible that what the Magi saw was actually similar to something the prophet Ezekiel witnessed hundreds of years earlier.

When God brought Israel out of Egypt, His desire was not merely to set His people free from slavery. He actually wanted to dwell in their midst. He wanted a covenant people who would provide Him a "house" on the earth. God told Moses, "Let them make Me a sanctuary, that I may dwell among them" (Exodus 25:8). God gave specific instructions for the building of His Tabernacle. Once finished, the manifest presence of God, the Shekinah glory, took up residence in the innermost chamber called the Holy of Holies.

Many years later, King Solomon built the Temple. Once again, God's Shekinah glory filled the temple in a dramatic fashion.

"When Solomon had finished praying, fire came down from heaven and consumed the burnt offering and the sacrifices; and the glory of the Lord filled the temple. And the priests could not enter the house of the Lord, because the glory of the Lord had filled the Lord's house. When all the children of Israel saw how the fire came down, and the glory of the Lord on the temple, they bowed their faces to the ground on the pavement, and worshiped and praised the Lord, saying: 'For He is good, For His mercy endures forever.'" —2 Chronicles 7:1-3

The glory of God rested in the Holy of Holies in Solomon's temple for hundreds of years, but Israel continued to sin and rebel. The time for judgment was approaching when Israel would be captured and looted. The Babylonians would destroy Solomon's temple and take the children of Israel away into captivity (which is the time Daniel's story took place). Before the temple was destroyed and before any physical devastation had taken place in the natural, something far more tragic had already happened. The glory of God departed from the temple. It left so quietly that most of Israel never even noticed, but the prophet Ezekiel saw it (Ezekiel 10). He described the progression as the glory of God moved one step at a time from the Holy of Holies to the threshold of the temple, then out of the temple through the eastern gate and on to the Mount of Olives. Finally, it was gone.

What a tragedy. God's manifest presence was no longer dwelling in the midst of His people. The physical destruction of Solomon's temple and the conquering of the nation were merely outward manifestations of their spiritual bankruptcy.

More than 100 years later the prophet Malachi said,

"'Behold, I send My messenger, and he will prepare the way before Me. And the Lord, whom you seek, will suddenly come to His temple, even the Messenger of the covenant, in whom you delight. Behold, He is coming,' says the Lord of hosts."   *—Malachi 3:1*

What a prophecy! God would send His messenger to His temple. This meant that the Messiah would come to a rebuilt temple. God promised restoration for the people, the land and the temple. In fact, the prophet Haggai declared, "The glory of this latter temple shall be greater than the former…" (Haggai 2:9). According to Haggai, this second temple was supposed to be the greater temple with a greater glory, but there was a problem.

When the foundation for the second temple was laid by the exiles, and those old enough to remember the first temple saw it, they began to weep out loud

(Ezra 3:12). It was so small and modest compared to the original. The physical beauty and grandeur of the second temple would pale in comparison to the first, but there was a much bigger problem. When the second temple was dedicated, God's glory did not return. Fire did not fall from heaven, as it had in the first temple. There was no manifestation of the Shekinah glory. They did not even have the ark of the covenant. God had restored some of His people to the land, but He did not take up residence with them.

Although the physical building had been erected, the presence of God that gave it purpose and meaning was still missing. The prophecies were unfulfilled. Israel was still waiting for its Messiah and for the return of God's glory. This is where we return to the star of Bethlehem.

It is interesting that when Ezekiel saw the glory of the Lord departing from the first temple, he could actually trace the movement of the departing glory as it went step-by-step. I think this sounds remarkably similar to what the shepherds saw when the angels appeared and announced the Savior's birth: "The glory of the Lord shone around them" (Luke 2:9). It sounds even more similar to what the Magi saw that allowed them to trace the moving of the "star" to a precise residential address. A natural heavenly body could never provide such precision or stand still over a particular house (Matthew 2:9). Could it be that the Magi actually saw the once-departed Shekinah glory of God now returning to Israel?

Jesus came into the world as the ultimate "Shekinah," the ultimate dwelling of God among men. This is why the Scriptures said that He would be called "Immanuel," which means "God with us!" (Isaiah 7:14). No wonder multitudes of angels announced His birth and worshiped God! Such a marvel the earth had never known. No spectacle of creation or human invention could compare to the miracle that God wrapped Himself in human flesh and made His home among us. John says that, "The Word became flesh and dwelt among us" (John 1:14). When we celebrate Christmas, we are literally celebrating the fact that God came to live among us. What an amazing thought!

"Christ, by highest heaven adored;
Christ, the everlasting Lord;
Late in time behold him come,
Offspring of a virgin's womb.
Veiled in flesh the Godhead see;
Hail the incarnate Deity,
Pleased as man with men to dwell,
Jesus, our Emmanuel.
Hark the herald angels sing
Glory to the newborn King."

("Hark the Herald Angels Sing" Charles Wesley, 1739)

SECTION V:

GIFTS FOR A KING

We three kings of Orient are;
Bearing gifts we traverse afar,
Field and fountain, moor and mountain,
Following yonder star.

O star of wonder, star of night,
Star with royal beauty bright,
Westward leading, still proceeding,
Guide us to thy perfect light.

Born a King on Bethlehem's plain
Gold I bring to crown Him again,
King forever, ceasing never,
Over us all to reign.

Frankincense to offer have I;
Incense owns a Deity nigh;
Prayer and praising, voices raising,
Worshiping God on high.

Myrrh is mine, its bitter perfume
Breathes a life of gathering gloom;
Sorr'wing, sighing, bleeding, dying,
Sealed in the stone-cold tomb.

Glorious now behold Him arise;
King and God and sacrifice;
Alleluia, Alleluia
Sounds through the earth and skies.

("We Three Kings" John Henry Hopkins, Jr., 1857)

The Old Testament declared that Gentiles from around the world would come to the Messiah bearing gifts that actually included gold and frankincense (Psalm 72:10-15; Isaiah 60:1-6). When the Magi from the East visited Jesus, they partly fulfilled this prophecy. The nations were indeed paying their respects to the great Jewish king, even bringing gold, frankincense and myrrh to honor Him. These gifts carried powerful prophetic meaning.

GOLD

Gold had great value in Jesus' day as it does in ours. It would have been a wonderful financial blessing for Galilean peasants who probably had very little. Some scholars have suggested that this financial gift may have funded the flight of Mary, Joseph and Jesus into Egypt to escape Herod's murderous rampage.

But in addition to its obvious practical use, gold was a gift for kings, and the Magi had come to meet the greatest King of all. The Messiah that Daniel foretold was to be a great King that would rule over the whole earth.

"I was watching in the night visions, and behold, One like the Son of Man, coming with the clouds of heaven! He came to the Ancient of Days, and they brought Him near before Him. Then to Him was given dominion and glory and a kingdom, that all peoples, nations, and languages should serve Him. His dominion is an everlasting dominion, which shall not pass away, and His kingdom the one which shall not be destroyed." —*Daniel 7:13, 14*

It is no wonder the Magi would have been eager to meet the Jewish Messiah and honor Him with gold. According to Daniel, the greatest prophet they had ever known, this "Son of Man," would come with the clouds of Heaven. He would be served by all the people of the earth, from every nation and language.

Babylonian and Persian kings had sometimes been given the title "King of Kings," but they had all died, and their kingdoms had passed away. Yet, Daniel's "Son of Man" would receive an eternal Kingdom with unlimited dominion and glory. That great monarch would be immortal and indestructible. Truly, this was to be the King of all kings and the Lord of all lords; that is why they came with gold. They had no more valuable resource to worship the highest-ranking King of all time and eternity.

FRANKINCENSE AND MYRRH

Frankincense and Myrrh are both resins (or gums) that come from the sap of trees. Frankincense comes from the Boswellia tree and myrrh from the Commiphora tree. Both substances are edible and fragrant with multiple purposes, the most practical of which are medicinal. Probably the most obvious reason these gifts were given to a baby was to care for Him and to treat any potential ailments, scrapes and bruises. They reveal a very tender side of the Magi. They had not come simply to pay respects out of dutiful reverence. These were heartfelt gifts of care and love. They had come to worship.

Prophetically, we can see even deeper meaning to these gifts. Frankincense and myrrh were gifts often presented to the gods. In the East, as well as Egypt, Rome and many other places, frankincense was used in religious ceremonies as part of the recipe for aromatic incense. The Magi probably had no idea that it was also used by the Jews in temple worship as a fragrant offering to God.

The Messiah predicted by Daniel and expected by these Magi was clearly an extraordinary person. In fact, He could not be considered a mere mortal at all. The person described by Daniel was nothing less than God-man. Daniel called Him, "The Son of Man," a title Jesus often used for Himself, identifying Himself as both human and divine.

Somehow, the Magi understood that Jesus was more than a man and even more than a king. They had not come merely to esteem a great king, but to worship the divine King. In Scripture, neither mortals nor angels are permitted to receive worship. Jesus was greater than a man, and He was greater than the angels. He was and is the unique and eternal Son of God.

BORN TO DIE

Frankincense and Myrrh were also used in ancient times to prepare bodies for burial. The emperor Nero once burned an entire harvest of frankincense at the funeral of one of his favorite mistresses. When Jesus was buried, His body was covered in burial spices, including myrrh.

If Daniel was indeed the source of the Magi's knowledge, they may have known that Jesus was destined to die for His people. Daniel had prophesied this, announcing that Messiah would be killed or "cut off, but not for Himself" (Daniel 9:26). Other prophets foretold this as well. Isaiah said,

"...For He was cut off from the land of the living; for the transgressions of My people He was stricken. And they made His grave with the wicked—but with the rich at His death, because He had done no violence, nor was any deceit in His mouth."   *—Isaiah 53:8, 9*

David prophesied the crucifixion of Jesus with stunning detail. In Psalm 22, he mentioned Jesus' rejection and scorn, the piercing of His hands and feet, the Roman soldiers' gambling for his clothes, and even His last words.

Daniel's words about the Messiah's death stood firmly in the tradition of the Old Testament prophets. Remarkably, it seems that God invited the Gentile Magi, as followers of Daniel's legacy, into that prophetic tradition. Perhaps the Magi brought frankincense and myrrh because they knew from Daniel's prophecies that the infant King of the Jews was destined to die. Or maybe their gift was more of an unconscious prophetic sign. Just as Mary of Bethany was unaware that her anointing of Jesus prepared Him for burial (Mark 14:8), so the Magi could have been unaware of the full meaning of their gifts. The Bible does not tell us their motive. One thing is certain; Jesus was born to die. From the beginning, His purpose was to "give his life a ransom for many" (Matthew 20:28).

In John 12:27, just before Jesus went to the cross, He said, "Now My soul is troubled, and what shall I say? 'Father, save Me from this hour?' But for this purpose I came to this hour." Jesus lived with an awareness of His purpose. He was born to die.

Nails, spear shall pierce him through
The cross be borne for me, for you.
Hail, hail the Word made Flesh,
The Babe, the Son of Mary!

("What Child is This" William Chatterton Dix, 1865)

SECTION VI:

HIS INDESCRIBABLE GIFT

The Bible reports the exact gifts the Magi presented to Jesus because each one was important and prophetic. Yet, as profound as those three gifts were, Christmas is not just about the Magi's gifts to Jesus, and it is not about our gifts to each other. It is not even about our gifts to God. The real significance of Christmas is what God gave to us: His only Son and the only gift that would cost Him something.

Whenever we talk about the cross and about salvation, we usually either focus on the transactional or judicial elements. In other words, we talk about how God paid the price that we couldn't pay and bought our salvation. That's the transactional part. Or we talk about how justice demanded that someone be punished for our sins, so Jesus took our place and received the punishment on our behalf. That's the judicial part.

These are great truths, but if we merely analyze and reduce them to doctrines, we will miss the visceral reality of the Father giving His only Son. To understand the cross, we do not need a theological degree. We need an honest look into the raw realities of love and life. If we know what it means to feel pain, what it feels like to lose something precious, give sacrificially, or love selflessly, then we can begin to relate, in a small way, to what God did. He gave us what was most precious, costly and painful to Him.

Think about this. What gift could God give that would show you His love? If God gave you a million dollars, you would appreciate it, but it wouldn't cost God anything. He can make a million dollars with a snap of His fingers. If God gave you a planet, it would cost Him nothing. If He gave you an entire galaxy, it would be effortless. He spoke the worlds into being. But when God gave us His Son, heaven went bankrupt.

When the angels announced the birth of Christ, they declared peace on earth and goodwill to men (Luke 2:14). This phrase has been used so much that it has become cliché, but these are some of the most important words that have ever been uttered. The coming of Jesus was a message from God: the ultimate expression of His love and goodwill toward us.

One of my favorite verses is Romans 8:32: "He who did not spare His own Son, but delivered Him up for us all, how shall He not with Him also freely give us all things?" In that verse, Apostle Paul points to the Cross as the ultimate proof of God's goodwill toward man. If God would give His only Son to us, if He would allow Him to suffer and die in our place, to be wounded, bruised and broken for us, we can be sure that He will give us anything else that we need.

With that one gift, God gave everything He had and everything we need. It was the one gift in which all other gifts are contained. Ephesians 1:3 says that

God has blessed us with EVERY spiritual blessing IN CHRIST! There is one thing God has to say and one gift Heaven has to give: Jesus! When you receive Jesus, you receive every gift of God, because EVERYTHING God has to give is in Christ!

THE FATHER'S ONLY SON

There once was a very wealthy man who was the heir of several generations of wealthy men before him, and each had increased the family fortune. This particular man had invested in art. He had the most valuable private holding in the world: Picasso, Rembrandt, Monet, Dali…works by some of the greatest artists in history. On his massive estate, he built a special wing of his mansion just to display his favorite pieces.

One day, the man met a beautiful woman. They fell in love and were married. Soon, his wife was pregnant with their first child. Life was a fairytale until the terrible day when she died giving birth to their first and only son. After the wife's death, it was just father and son. They became inseparable. It is impossible to express how much this father loved his son. They were best friends. They did everything together. The son was his father's whole world, more valuable than his vast wealth multiplied a million times over.

When the son grew up, he planned to take over the family business, but he felt he should first get experience outside of his familiar life. He joined the military and was shipped off to war. Though the son was thousands of miles away, he stayed close to his father by writing letters. He wrote faithfully every few days. The father awaited each letter with great anticipation. His butler knew how much those letters meant to him, so he would hand-deliver them the moment they arrived.

One day, the butler came into the father's study, holding one of the familiar envelopes from the battlefield. The father took the letter excitedly, but instantly noticed that something was different. His son's personal details and familiar handwriting were missing. This letter was from the son's commander. The father's hands trembled as he pulled the small piece of paper out and read the words he dreaded most. "Dear Sir, we regret to inform you that your son has been killed in the line of duty…" The father fell to his knees sobbing.

For weeks he was overcome with grief, not knowing how to go on, but one day, the father had an idea. He commissioned a local artist to paint a portrait of his son. He rearranged his art gallery to make room for it. Right in the middle of the gallery, set higher than all other paintings, hung the portrait that the father named "The Son." Out of all the priceless works of art, "The Son" was the father's favorite. He would make a special trip to the gallery every day to look at it and remember his beloved son. Tears would stream down his face as he thought about the one that he loved so much. All the other paintings, though priceless to the world, seemed worthless to him.

Eventually, the father died also. Since he had no living heir, the estate was to be auctioned off. When auction day arrived, wealthy investors from around the world, especially art collectors, arrived to secure their prized piece of the estate.

The auctioneer opened by announcing that they would begin with the piece titled "The Son." The name of the artist was unknown, and the buyers stirred restlessly as the auctioneer began. "We will start the bidding at $1,000. Can I get $1,000?" At the back of the crowd one hand went into the air: the butler's. He was not a wealthy man and could never afford a Picasso or Rembrandt, but he had no interest in them anyway. He only wanted this portrait of his master's son. He had seen the son grow from a little boy into a man and had come to love him as his own. "I'll give $1,000," he said. The auctioneer continued, "Can I get $1,500?" No hands went up. "Can I get $1,200? $1,100?" By now, the wealthy buyers began to mumble and complain. This is not what they had come for. They only came for the valuable pieces. The auctioneer was wasting their precious time with bids on a worthless portrait. "Going once, going twice… sold!" The gavel came down; the butler came forward to claim his purchase.

Then the auctioneer announced, "And with this purchase, the auction comes to a conclusion. Thank you all for coming out today." The wealthy collectors started to shout, "What about the paintings, the cars, the house, the property? What about the rest of the estate?" The auctioneer explained, "I am sorry to disappoint you, but the father gave very specific instruction in his will regarding the sale of his possessions. He required that the auction start by offering "The Son." And 'whoever takes the son gets everything.'"

When God gave His Son to us, He gave us His everything: His entire estate. That is the message of Christmas. Those who receive God's Son receive all the treasures of heaven. For those that reject Him, God has nothing else to offer.

Sinners, wrung with true repentance,
Doomed for guilt to endless pains,
Justice now revokes the sentence,
Mercy calls you; break your chains.
Come and worship, come and worship,
Worship Christ, the newborn King.

("Angels from the Realms of Glory" James Montgomery, 1816)

SECTION VII:

WHAT DOES THIS ALL MEAN?

The Magi left everything behind and traveled to a distant land to find the One foretold by Daniel and the prophets of old. Their gifts recognized him as God, as King and as heaven's indescribable gift to us. Amazingly, they somehow knew the hour of their visitation, even when Israel missed it. They had not yet seen His miracles or heard His teachings. They did not possess all the Scriptures telling of Messiah's death, resurrection and future return. Yet, as heirs of Daniel's legacy, they believed God and worshipped His Son, the Messiah. They were truly "wise men" in the ultimate sense, signaling that, one day, people from every tribe and nation would stream to the King of the Jews. Therefore, Scripture has immortalized their astounding faith. They are now a powerful example to us, thousands of years later. Their story takes us beyond the traditional Nativity Scene into the real Christmas story. God is still drawing men and women from "far off" to be brought near through the blood of Christ.

Let me take a moment to address the person reading this book who might not know Jesus as their Savior. You might think of yourself as an unlikely candidate to receive God's mercy and love. Maybe you feel "far away" from God. If that is the case, the story of the Magi should resonate in your heart. The message we find in the story of the Magi is that God is drawing men and women from afar. The door has been open wide. Salvation is available, not only to those who are "kosher", but to anyone who will call upon the name of Jesus. Ephesians 2:13 says, "But now in Christ Jesus you who once were far away have been brought near by the blood of Christ." You don't need to traverse a thousand miles to find God. He already sent His Son from Heaven to earth to find you. All you need to do is to repent and believe the Gospel. And what is the Gospel?

1. We are all guilty before God. The Bible says that all have sinned and fallen short of the glory of God (Romans 3:23. We have all gone astray (Isaiah

53:6). There is no one righteous (Romans 3:10). The heart of man is deceitful and desperately wicked (Jeremiah 17:9). And we cannot save ourselves through good works (Ephesians 2:8-9)

2. Because of our sins, we were become by nature enemies of God (Colossians 1:21, Romans 5:10) and separated from God (Isaiah 59:2)

3. But Jesus died and shed His blood to reconcile us unto God (Colossians 1:20, 2 Corinthians 5:18, Romans 5:8-9)

4. There is no other way to come to God except through Jesus (John 14:6)

5. By turning from sin and self-righteousness (our own goodness) and putting our trust in Jesus and His death on the cross, we can be saved. (Romans 10:9, Acts 16:31)

If that's your desire, I would like to invite you to pray a simple prayer like this one:

"Father God, I come to you in the name of Jesus. I confess that I am a sinner. I cannot save myself, but I throw myself upon your mercy. I confess with my mouth what I believe in my heart – that Jesus my Lord, that He died for me and rose from the dead. I put my trust in Him for my salvation. Jesus Christ, Son of God, save me now. Have mercy upon me. Give me a new heart. Be my Savior, my Lord and my very best friend. I give you my whole life from this day forward. In Jesus name. Amen.

ABOUT THE AUTHOR

Daniel Kolenda is a modern missionary evangelist who has led more than 19-million people to Christ face-to-face through massive open-air evangelistic campaigns in some of the most dangerous, difficult and remote locations on earth. As the successor to world renowned Evangelist Reinhard Bonnke, Daniel is the president and CEO of Christ for All Nations; a ministry which has conducted some of the largest evangelistic events in history, has published over 190 million books in 104 languages and has offices in 10 nations around the world. He also hosts an internationally syndicated television program.

Daniel is a gifted, fifth-generation preacher whose ministry is marked by a powerful evangelistic anointing and incredible miracles after the model of Jesus; preaching, teaching and healing. The blind receive their sight, the lame walk, the lepers are cleansed, and the deaf hear — he has even seen the dead raised — but most importantly, the poor have the gospel preached to them. It is this single minded Gospel emphasis that makes the ministry of Daniel Kolenda and Christ for all Nations so unique.

Daniel is a graduate of Southeastern University on Lakeland, Florida and the Brownsville Revival School of Ministry in Pensacola, Florida, but his greatest education has come from the years of ministry side-by-side with his mentor and spiritual father Evangelist Reinhard Bonnke. Together they have circled the globe preaching the Gospel and continue to do so as a single-minded team with great effectiveness.

As a previous successful pastor and church planter Daniel holds a tireless commitment, and dedication to the Church. More than half of the cost of every evangelistic campaign is invested in a "follow-up" system to see every convert become a faith-filled, fearless, disciple of Christ and member of a local church.

Daniel, with his wife Rebekah and their children, Elijah, Gloria, London, and Lydia reside in the Orlando area.

Visit DanielKolenda.com

NOTES

NOTES

NOTES

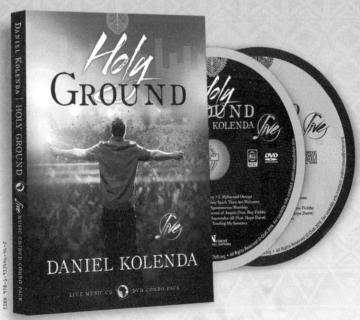

BY HIS STRIPES WE ARE HEALED
ISAIAH 53:5

CFAN.ORG

ANOINTING OIL FROM ISRAEL

This anointing oil comes on a keychain so that you are always ready to pray for the sick according to James 5:14.

Handmade in Jerusalem, Israel of authent olive wood. Comes with a Frankincense & Myrrh anointing oil direct from the Holy La

ITEM # OIL001

For your gift of $12 or more